CAPE TOWN

CAPE TOWN

Jean Morris
Text: Jessica Abrahams

Published by Don Nelson
Cape Town 1979

First edition 1979
Second edition 1981

ISBN 0 909238 63 4
Designed by Peter Ibbotson.
Photoset by McManus Bros. (Pty) Ltd., Cape Town.
Lithographic Reproduction by Hirt & Carter (Pty) Ltd., Cape Town.
Printed by Printpak (Cape) Ltd., Cape Town.

Acknowledgements

Although the bulk of the photography for this book was done by Jean Morris, several other photographers have been involved, and a list appears at the end of the book. We would like to thank Glynn Griffiths, Geraldine Farley, Paul Lindenberg and Clyde Davidson for their contributions, which have helped to make the book a comprehensive mosaic of Cape Town and its surrounding areas.

The following sources have proved particularly useful in assembling information for the text and captions: *South Africa* by Gerald Cubitt and Arnold Helfet (Struik); and two books by T.V. Bulpin, *Discovering Southern Africa* (Books of Africa) and *Southern Africa: Land of Beauty and Splendour* (Readers' Digest Association).

We are also most grateful to Captour (Cape Tourism Authority) for their generous assistance with information and photographs, and in particular we would like to thank Clyde Davidson and Liza Thynne for their help and advice.

The Cape of Good Hope in 1700. (Cape Archives)

HISTORICAL SKETCH OF THE CAPE

The history of Cape Town is really the beginning point of history for the whole country, as this was the site of the earliest European settlement on the sub-continent, and ever since has been a 'Tavern of the Seas' for passing ships. Cape Town is appropriately known as the Mother City of South Africa.

Voyages of Exploration and Discovery

The earliest stirrings of exploration from Europe towards the Southern part of Africa were originally prompted by economical considerations and the realization that it might be possible to establish a safe sea route to the East. It was the fifteenth century, the beginning of the Age of Discovery, and patrons such as Prince Henry ('the Navigator') and King John of Portugal were encouraging voyages of exploration to distant lands in order to increase European knowledge of the world, to colonise and trade with new countries and also to spread Christianity.

It was under the patronage of King John of Portugal that in 1488 Bartholomew Diaz, with three ships, rounded what he called the 'Cabo Tormentoso' ('Cape of Storms') and sailed on as far east as Port Alfred before turning back. On the return voyage, he visited the Cape, which he had passed in a storm on the way out, and planted a stone cross, or *padrão*, dedicated to St Phillip. On Diaz's return to Portugal, King John, realizing the potential of the new landfall, renamed it 'Cabo de Boa Esperanza' ('Cape of Good Hope').

The first person to reach the East via the Cape was Vasco da Gama, who was commissioned by King Manuel 1 of Portugal. In 1497 he rounded the Cape with four ships, eventually reaching Calicut, India, before returning to Portugal. In 1503 Table Bay was visited and named 'Agoeda de Saldanha' ('the watering place of Saldanha')

Prince Henry the Navigator (1394 - 1460), one of the Portuguese monarchs who encouraged exploration of the unknown oceans and continents. (Cape Archives)

by Antonio da Saldanha, who mistakenly thought he had rounded the Cape. While here he climbed and named Table Mountain and was thus the first white person to see its incredible view of two oceans. A hundred years later, Table

Portion of a *padrão*. These were stone crosses erected by the Portuguese explorers to mark their travels. (Cape Archives)

Right: Meeting of Jan van Riebeeck and the Hottentots at the foot of Devil's Peak. (Cape Archives)

Below: Ground plan of the Castle of Good Hope, drawn in 1793. (Cape Archives)

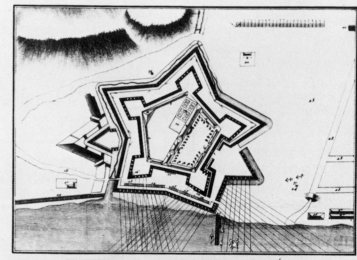

PLAN DE LA CITADELLE DU CAP DE BONNE ESPÉRANCE.
Levé sur les Lieux en 1793, par L. De Grand-Pré.

Bay was renamed by the Dutch admiral, Joris van Spilbergen, who transferred the original name to a bay some 100 km up the west coast.

The first permanent settlement

In those early years the Cape was used as anchorage by Portuguese, Dutch and British ships, but no permanent settlement existed until the powerful Dutch East India Company, established in 1602, issued a mandate to one Johan Anthonie van Riebeeck, a young ship's surgeon, to establish a settlement which could provide passing ships with fresh meat (traded from the natives), fruit and vegetables (to be grown by the settlers) and also, when necessary, with shelter and hospital services. He was also to maintain friendly relations with the natives.

In 1652, Van Riebeeck, the first Commander of the Cape, arrived in Table Bay with a fleet of three ships. He commenced building an earth fortification near the beach – the first permanent European structure to be erected on the sub-continent, replaced in 1666 with a pentagonal stone-built fortress, the Castle of Good Hope, which still houses the military headquarters of the Cape.

By 1657 Van Riebeeck was finding the produce of his 'Company Garden' insufficient to supply the Company's ships, so he released some of his soldiers and allotted land to them along the Liesbeek River near Rondebosch. These early farmers were known as 'free burghers'.

With the appointment of Simon van der Stel as second Commander of the Cape in 1679, and his promotion in 1691 to Governor of the Cape, the settlement began expanding into the interior. By the end of the century Stellenbosch had been founded by Van der Stel, and a group of French Huguenot immigrants had settled in the Franschhoek, Paarl and Drakenstein areas. The arrival of the Huguenots with their specialized agricultural knowledge marked the beginning of the Cape wine industry proper, although the first wine had been pressed as early as 1659. French ancestry can be remarked in such family names as Du Toit, De Villiers, Le Roux, Malherbe, Joubert and others.

The next Governor of the Cape Colony, Wilhelm Adriaan van der Stel, encouraged exploration further into the interior in search of water and grazing for cattle, where his father had been content that the colony should be confined by the first mountain ranges and that its activities should be mainly agricutural. Wilhelm Adriaan was, however, dismissed after Stellenbosch farmers complained about his unfair control of the market for farm produce.

As a result of this, sponsored immigration from Europe was stopped, and the additional manpower necessary for catering to the needs of passing ships was provided in the form of slave labour. These slaves, who originated from Malaya and other eastern countries, Madagascar and West Africa, formed an increasingly large sector of the population, and together with the mainly illegitimate offspring of mixed parentage, eventually merged into the group known as the Cape Coloureds.

The Cape changes hands – several times

The early eighteenth century saw settlers moving as far inland as Tulbagh ('The Land of Waveren') and the beginning of such new industries as the tobacco industry. It also saw the appointment of the first South African-born Governor, Hendrik Swellengrebel, in 1739. It was in the latter half of the eighteenth century that the colonists, moving steadily inland east and north, first came into contact with the Africans who had come down from the North. Both groups were basically moving in order to find the same things: water and grazing for their cattle, and this conflict of interests provoked several wars and effectively halted for a time the expansion of the colonists.

At the same time the Cape was embarking on a career of frequent changes of control which was to continue for more than thirty years. In 1781 a French garrison was sent to aid the Cape in case of British attack. Then in 1795 the Prince of Orange, who had gone into exile in Britain when his country became the Batavian Republic under revolutionary France instructed the colonists to surrender to the British forces, which they did, after the Battle of Muizenberg. General Craig became the first British Governor. After eight years the Cape was returned to the Dutch by the Treaty of Amiens, but when war with Napoleon broke out again, the British occupied the Cape once more after the Battle of Blaauberg. The Cape was finally ceded to the British in 1814 and Lord Charles Somerset assumed the Governorship.

As most of the population was not British, a policy of 'Anglicization' was implemented to enforce the use of English in Government departments, law courts, churches and schools, ostensibly to facilitate communication. This was of course badly received by the public. In 1820, however, 5 000 British immigrants arrived at Port Elizabeth, and after this the tension of the situation was somewhat eased.

The British brought about a more orderly and systematic rule at the Cape, which was now a Crown Colony, and initated or encouraged various new public services, such as a mail packet service to and from Britain in 1815; the Public Library service in 1818; the Royal Observatory (now the South African Astronomical Observatory) in 1820; the first lighthouse, erected at Mouille Point, and the road through Franschhoek Pass, both in 1824.

The Great Trek

From 1836 to 1838 groups of farmers dissatisfied with British rule left their homes and migrated inland and northwards in search of an independent territory. These pioneers were responsible for the original settling of the areas which became known as the Transvaal, Orange Free State and Natal, though a small group of English traders had been established in Natal in 1824 at the port of Durban.

At the same time, the colonists who had remained behind at the Cape were not entirely satisfied with the British system of rule, and made determined efforts to obtain a representative form of government. At first their efforts were only partially successful: in 1834 the partly-nominated Legislative Council of the Cape was formed. In 1854 this became an elected Parliament with an Executive of British officials, and by 1872 the Cape had a fully responsible government.

Riches in the North

Progress and development in the Cape in the nineteenth century were greatly accelerated by the discovery of diamonds and gold further inland. The first diamonds were discovered near Hopetown in 1866, with subsequent discoveries of diamond-rich deposits along the Vaal River and around the town of Kimberley in the Cape. Gold was first discovered in 1870 in the Murchison Range in the Transvaal. One of the effects of these discoveries was to attract many people to try to make their fortunes in the gold and diamond fields of South Africa. Many of these odd and interesting characters passed through Cape Town on their way north, and some left lasting marks to remind us of them.

One such was Cecil John Rhodes, who was elected Prime Minister of the Cape in 1890 and left his estates to the nation. His home on the Groote Schuur estate has been used as the Prime Minister's residence ever since, and also on this

Above: Greenmarket Square with the Town House in 1762, by Johannes Rach. The square took its name from vegetable stalls such as the one in the foreground. (Cape Archives)

Below: Groot Constantia in the early nineteenth century. The magnificent oaks are already well established in this picture. (Cape Archives)

Above: Cape Town in 1849 – a panoramic view from the summit of the Lutheran Church in Strand Street by Capt Walter Stanhope Sherwill. (Cape Archives)

Left: Lieutenant-General Lord Charles Henry Somerset (1767 - 1831), First British governor of the Cape. (Cape Archives)

Below: St Stephen's Church, built in 1799, was Cape Town's first theatre (The African Theatre) but after 1839 it was used as a church, the only Dutch Reformed Church to be named after a saint. (Cape Archives)

large estate were established the University of Cape Town and Groote Schuur Hospital, one of the most renowned hospitals and medical schools in the world. Another bequest was the property named Kirstenbosch on the eastern slopes of Table Mountain, on which has been established a botanical garden that has become world famous.

Some of the developments taking place around this time were the construction of the first railway line from Cape Town to Wellington which was begun in 1859; Table Bay Docks, which were begun in 1860; and the telegraph system between Cape Town and Simonstown which was started in 1865. Cape Town was linked to Europe by cable via Cairo in 1879, and the railway link between Cape Town and Johannesburg, the metropolis that had sprung up on the gold fields of the Witwatersrand, was completed in 1892.

Independence

In 1910 South Africa became a self-governing Union by the South Africa Act, under which the country was given three different capitals: Cape Town being the legislative capital, Pretoria in the Transvaal being the administrative capital, and Bloemfontein in the Orange Free State being the judicial capital. Finally in 1961 South Africa became a fully independent Republic.

In these, and further, national developments, Cape Town, being the Mother City and legislative capital, has of course been closely involved, yet despite this she has remained unique and individual, with a special quality which cannot be defined, a magic which owes something to her proud heritage of British and Dutch ancestry; something to her ever-cosmopolitan, ever-changing population, as visitors come and go, or, captivated, stay; and something to her breathtaking natural beauty, which caused Sir Francis Drake, who passed the Cape in 1580 on his way around the globe in the 'Golden Hind', to say: 'It is a most stately thing and the fairest Cape in the whole circumference of the earth.'

PHYSICAL STRUCTURE

The Cape Peninsula was originally a pair of islands divided by a short stretch of sea at Fishhoek Valley. Geologically, the Cape System originated in three sedimentary layers which were deposited successively: a base layer, the Table Mountain series, of quartzite and sandstone, in which are found hard pebbles scratched by glacial ice; next, the Bokkeveld series, of mudstones, shales and sandstones, rich in fossils; and lastly the Witteberg series, consisting of thin bands of quartzite, sandy shale and the remains of plants.

Under the weight of these deposits, however,

the mantle of the earth first collapsed and then rose in successive arches and troughs, bent, twisted and folded by the tremendous pressures exerted on them. Heavy erosion took place, forming deep valleys and kloofs, and leaving features such as Table Mountain exposed. Thus was created the spectacular mountainous region which delights travellers with breathtaking views and has taxed the ingenuity of road engineers to the utmost!

The climate of the Cape is basically Mediterranean, with hot, dry summers and cool, wet winters. On the whole the climate is moderate, with snow almost unknown in the Peninsula.

The prevailing winter wind is the North-Wester which brings rain, and in summer the fierce South-Easter blows, known locally as the 'Cape Doctor' because it blows away dust and pollution. The South-Easter is also responsible for an unusual phenomenon: on encountering the Peninsula mountain chain, the moisture-laden South-East wind from over False Bay is forced to rise. The moisture condenses into a thick white cloud which spills over the level top of the front of the mountain and disappears as it hits the higher temperatures of the air lower down. This cap of cloud is known as the 'table cloth'.

According to legend, however, the 'table cloth' was originally produced by a retired pirate named Van Hunks who had a smoking contest with the devil on the slopes of the mountain (hence the name 'Devil's Peak') which lasted several days and enveloped the mountain in a cloud of smoke. This contest is repeated from time to time, as can be seen!

The vegetation of the Peninsula is varied: there are still pockets of indigenous Cape Forest in deep kloofs, on top of and on the eastern slopes of Table Mountain. For the remainder, the basic indigenous vegetation is known as 'fynbos', and consists of small hardy shrubs and plants which are able to withstand the sometimes harsh conditions, including mild but regular droughts in summer.

In areas such as the Cape Flats, especially along the coast, the sand dunes form an entirely different environment from the Peninsula, and have their own typical dune vegetation, consisting mainly of small, hardy plants which can survive in nutrient-deficient sand and harsh, desiccating winds.

Despite the superficially uniform appearance of some of the vegetation, the Western Cape forms one of the six major floral kingdoms of the world, with some 16 000 species, while the Cape Peninsula, a botanist's paradise, has more

than 2 600 species, more than the whole of Great Britain. The wild flowers which bloom in spring are one of the natural wonders of the world.

The fauna of the Cape, apart from domestic animals, are rather scarce, as there is not much lush vegetation to support them. There are still baboons and dassies (rock rabbits) on the mountain, as well as a few Thars (Himalayan mountain goats) descended from a pair which escaped from the Groot Schuur zoo.

History has it that there used to be lions and leopards, buck, hippopotamus, and elephants too, but these have all long since disappeared.

Small buck such as Grysbok and even the occasional leopard are still found in the remoter areas of the Western Cape mountain ranges, but just about the only buck left on the Peninsula are the tame reindeer at Rhodes memorial. The area down at the tip of the Peninsula has now been demarcated as the Cape of Good Hope Nature Reserve, in an attempt to preserve the indigenous fauna as well as flora of the Cape.

THE CITY

Visitors to the Cape are often confused by the preconception that the City of Cape Town is at the 'bottom' of the African continent and therefore faces southwards out across the Atlantic. In fact the long axis of the Peninsula lies basically in a north-south orientation, with the city practically at the northenmost point, facing north across Table Bay towards Robben Island with its lighthouse and convict settlement, and the rest of the African continent; and with Cape Point, the meeting place of the Atlantic and Indian Oceans, about 50 km south of the city.

The most familiar landmark in the Peninsula is Table Mountain, which was named in 1503 by Antonio da Saldanha, the first European to climb it. It can be seen as far as 200 km out to sea, and has almost come to symbolise Cape Town.

The front of the mountain, rising in a sheer, rocky precipice to the characteristic 'table top', together with the satellite arms of Devil's Peak, Lion's Head and Signal Hill, form a gently-curving horseshoe in which nestles the city. Behind this familiar backdrop, the mountain extends down the west coast of the Peninsula from Camps Bay to Llandudno in a series of buttresses known as the Twelve Apostles, and also forms a plateau to the south of the front table on which are situated several reservoirs which supply water to the city.

There are many walking and climbing routes up the mountain, but it is highly inadvisable for anyone to attempt to reach the top without a reliable guide. At the western end of the front

Left: Table Mountain from the old Camp Ground in Rondebosch.

Right: Newlands Avenue towards the end of the nineteenth century.

table there is an aerial cableway which provides a far safer means of ascent, and at the top there are lookout points with superb views, and an old stone-built tearoom. Easy walks can be taken on the level but rocky top of the mountain.

Another pleasant walk starts at Kloof Nek, the saddle between Table Mountain and Lion's Head, and skirts the mountain above Camps Bay. It is known as the 'Pipe Track' because it follows the course of the pipes carrying water from the reservoirs on top of the mountain to the filtration plant near the Nek.

The bay around which Cape Town has grown forms a natural harbour, but, facing north, it is open to the north-west gales of winter, and many is the old ship that lies wrecked on the bottom of Table Bay.

One of the most famous wrecks was that of the 'Jonge Thomas' in 1773 near the mouth of the Salt River. A local dairyman named Wolraad Woltemade who was passing by, rode his horse into the high seas, ferrying members of the crew to safety. He was eventually overwhelmed by the panicking crew and all were drowned. It is thought that Woltemade used to live in the old fisherman's cottage 'Klein Zoar' in Wymyss

Road, Brooklyn, which is now a national monument.

Table Bay Docks were begun in 1860. Nowadays practically nothing remains of the original harbour except the old Clock Tower in the Victoria Basin, believed to occupy the site of the Imhoff Battery, and which is now restored and used as a museum.

In 1905 it was decided that the harbour facilities were inadequate, and a project was initiated which eventually resulted in enlargement of the harbour as well as massive land reclamation, creating a 146 ha area of land behind the harbour. Thus the present Foreshore area used to be all under water, and Strand Street was so named because it was the nearest to the beach. The position of the old marine promenade can be seen by the line of old palm trees near the fountain at the bottom of Adderley Street.

One of the most popular attractions of the shorefront which was lost in the reclamation of the Foreshore was the old Pier. Opened in 1913 by Sir Frederic de Waal, the Pier was about 14 m wide and 300 m long, with a tower at the end of it. Entrance cost a penny, and there were

Left: Detail from an engraving depicting the bravery of Wolraad Woltemade at the wreck of the *'Jonge Thomas'*. (Cape Archives)

Below: Rogge Bay, about 1900. This area is now all reclaimed land. (Cape Archives)

additional attractions such as hired rowboats, boxing matches, orchestral concerts and so on.

The curving sweep of the harbour and the shoreline has now been partially obscured by the raised freeway skirting the lower areas of town, all built on reclaimed land. Many of these buildings are tall, ultra-modern structures, such as the towering B.P. Centre, and Sanlam Building, which was one of the first 'skyscrapers' to be built on the Foreshore and for several years used to display the news headlines and the time in moving lights along the top of the wall facing uptown.

Another building which stands where the ocean once lapped is the handsome Nico Malan Opera House and Theatre complex. It contains some of the most modern theatrical equipment in the world, and provides cultural entertainment of a high standard.

Higher up, the city is an interesting mixture of old and new. Although many of the quaint old customs have succumbed to progress, enough of them survive to make Cape Town as fascinating a place to live in as it is to visit. The Coloured and Malay flower sellers still harangue one without respite in the colourful Flower Parade in Adderley Street; and there are still open-air markets on the Grand Parade on Wednesday and Saturday mornings, where one can pick over piles of unashamed junk, or happily pay twice its actual value for a 'real bargain'.

The noon gun still frightens the pigeons and seagulls into flight every day, though this old muzzle-loading cannon, located on Signal Hill, is now fired electronically from the Observatory. The custom of firing the cannon at midday originated in 1902, and during the world wars signalled a two-minute silence of prayer for those at the front.

From the statue of Van Riebeeck (presented to the city in 1855 by Cecil John Rhodes) the Heerengracht runs straight towards the mountain, becoming Adderley Street beyond the entrance to the railway station. Adderley Street

Left: The Cape Town Pier, about 1920. The waterfront reaches approximately as high as the site of the present-day fountain in Adderley Street. (Cape Archives)

Above right: Entrance to the Pier. (Cape Archives)

Right: A view of the Groote Kerk, mother church of the Dutch Reformed Church, from Church Square in 1854. (Cape Archives)

itself was originally named 'Heerengracht', which means 'Gentlemen's Canal' in Dutch, and refers to the stream which originally ran down its centre in an open canal, to reach the sea more or less where the fountain now stands. Part of this water was led off along Darling Street (then called Keizersgracht) to form the moat around the Castle of Good Hope.

The Castle of Good Hope was built between 1666 and 1675 to replace the earth fortification erected by Van Riebeeck on his arrival, and is thus one of the oldest permanent structures in the Cape. It is built in the shape of a pentagonal star, the classical design of Dutch forts in the seventeenth century, and the bastions at the angles of the pentagon are named for the titles of the Prince of Orange: Leerdam, Buren, Oranje, Nassau, and Catzenellenbogen.

The gateway to the Castle has a pediment with the arms of the Dutch East India Company on it, and across the interior grounds is a defensive cross-wall (the Kat), which originally housed the

Governor and his staff. The ornamental Kat balcony was executed by Anton Anreith, and from it important proclamations were read and new governors sworn in. It now contains an interesting collection of paintings and antiques. The Castle also has a military and maritime museum.

At the top of Adderley Street stand several imposing and dignified buildings. The Groote Kerk is the mother church of the Dutch Reformed Church, and the oldest church in South Africa. Its pulpit was carved by Anton Anreith from a single stinkwood trunk. Across Bureau Street stands the old Supreme Court, which was once the Slave Lodge, and is now the Cultural History Museum. It still has the original well in the courtyard.

Next to this stand the Houses of Parliament, completed in 1884, containing the famous Parliamentary Library, which grew out of the collection of books, documents and original paintings and drawings devoted to the history of

Strand Street in 1852, from a watercolour by T. W. Bowler. (Cape Archives)

Wale Street, with the original building of St George's Cathedral, completed in 1834, on the right. (Cape Archives)

St George's Street in 1875. (Cape Archives)

South Africa which was bequeathed to the nation in 1917 by Sidney Mendelssohn, a wealthy diamond merchant of the early Kimberley days.

Beyond the Houses of Parliament stands Government House or Tuynhuys, begun in 1699 as a pleasure lodge for Governor Wilhelm Adriaan van der Stel, and now used as the State President's residence. Behind the Tuynhuys, facing onto Stal Square, is the Lodge De Goede Hoop, the oldest Masonic Lodge in South Africa. This building was a joint effort by Anton Anreith, Herman Schutte and Louis-Michel Thibault, three famous Cape architects of the late eighteenth and early nineteenth centuries. Across the way from the Houses of Parliament is the imposing Neo-Gothic-style stone cathedral of St George the Martyr which was designed by Sir Herbert Baker in 1901. Next to the cathedral is the South African Library, a reference library containing a particularly fine collection specializing in Africana.

These buildings all flank the beginning of Government Avenue, a 1 000 m oak-lined walk which bisects the original Company Gardens of Van Riebeeck. These gardens are no longer cultivated for agricultural purposes, and are known instead as the Botanical Gardens, containing a large collection of indigenous and exotic plants. The Avenue and Gardens provide a welcome haven in the centre of the city where office workers, shoppers and visitors can relax on shaded benches and watch the birds and playful squirrels.

Beyond the Botanical Gardens are the buildings of the National Art Gallery, the South African Museum and the small Jewish museum, which is housed in the original Gardens synagogue, built in 1862, the oldest synagogue in Southern Africa. Next to this stands the 'new' synagogue, built in 1905, whose twin towers can be seen rising from the sea of treetops.

The top end of Government Avenue is flanked by the Michaelis School of Fine Art, a faculty of the University of Cape Town, and Cape Town High School, on the grounds of which once stood the Hope Mill, one of five water mills which operated along the banks of the Fresh River until the municipality bought them all out in 1868. The main part of the river was dammed up at Silverstream above Tafelberg Road, but the overflow still follows the old course of the river, now mainly underground, down to the sea.

Other buildings of interest in the city include the Lutheran Church in Strand Street, built in 1774 by Martin Melck. It was erected as a 'store room' because no religion other than the Dutch Reformed Church was tolerated in the Cape at that time.

Across the road and a few blocks lower down is the Koopmans de Wet House, built in 1702 and named after the family who lived there in the early nineteenth century. It is now a historical monument, filled with period furniture and prints.

The Old Town House in Greenmarket Square, built in 1761, was originally the civic centre and council house of Cape Town until the present City Hall, a massive sandstone Italian-style structure, was built in 1905. The Old Town House now contains the Michaelis collection of early Dutch and Flemish paintings.

High up on Buitenkant Street stands Rust-en-Vreugd, a double-storied Roccoco-style town house with woodcarvings over the front door by Anton Anreith. Built in 1777, it was once used as a school, but is now restored and contains the William Fehr collection of watercolours.

Apart from these places which have been set aside as permanent monuments, walking through the city with an observant eye shows one a city filled with mementoes of by-gone days. Greenmarket Square, where teams of oxen once outspanned, is still cobbled and shaded by old Java Fig trees. A plaque still marks the site of the 'Slave Tree', under which slaves stood to be sold, and the old slave bell, which controlled the working hours of the slaves of the Dutch East India Company, still stands in the Company Gardens.

There are still areas of character and charm, such as the upper reaches of Long Street, crammed with second-hand and junk shops housed in the old Victorian buildings – some dilapidated, some brightly painted – and everywhere around town can be seen quaint old buildings, carefully preserved or restored, squeezed between the much taller and plainer modern blocks.

On the slopes of Signal Hill above the city lies the colourful area known as the Malay Quarter, though its actual name is Schotsche Kloof. The Malays are Muslims who came to the Cape as political prisoners and as slaves, bringing a culture which has become an inseparable part of Cape tradition: the Malay women are often seen going about their business dressed in graceful traditional saris, and one does not have to be Malay to enjoy the spicy delicacies such as samoosas and tammelytjies. In fact Malay cooking has become very much a part of traditional Cape cookery. And on still evenings, the voices of the muezzins can be heard, calling the faithful to prayer from the minarets of the mosques.

On top of Signal Hill is the *kramat* or tomb of Mahomed Gasan Gaibie Shah, a Muslim holy man; and in one of the restored Georgian houses at the top of Wale Street is a Malay museum containing relics and items typical of the Malay community.

In contrast to the bustling Malay Quarter, on the other side of the city, on the slopes of Devil's Peak lies District Six, so named because the city was originally divided into six districts for election purposes, but called Kanaladorp by the Malays. It was once a poor but lively Coloured community, particularly at New Year, when it became the nucleus of the colourful explosion known as the 'Coon Carnival'. In 1966 the area was 're-zoned' and the Coloured residents, amidst loud but ineffectual public sympathy, were forced to move to other areas. It was intended to 'clean up' the area, but this projected redevelopment has not yet been started, and the suburb, largely demolished, stands a barren monument to insensitive bureaucracy.

Above the commercial centre of the city, between the Malay Quarter and District Six, lie the residential suburbs of Gardens, Tamboerskloof, Higgo Vale, Oranjezicht, Vredehoek and Devil's Peak, which are densely populated because they are fairly well sheltered and conveniently close to town. Some of the oldest residences built in the Cape are to be found here, and a surprising number have partially or wholly survived, such as Welgemeend, the home of 'Onze Jan' Hofmeyr; Leeuwenhof, the residence of the Administrator of the Cape; Waterhof, an old U-shaped thatched farmhouse recently restored; and Rheezicht, a fine gabled homestead.

Malay women, about 1870. (Cape Archives)

The Mouille Point lighthouse was built in 1824. This watercolour was painted in about 1842. (Cape Archives)

THE CAPE PENINSULA

In a brief glance at the South Western Cape it may be difficult to grasp the amazing range of conditions which produce the wide variety of climates and environments. This can be partly understood by exploring the sea currents prevailing along its shores.

To the west the cold Benguela Current sweeps up from the Antarctic to hit Africa at the Cape with a temperature of about 10°C. This current influences the whole of the west coast of Africa, but on the eastern seaboard the warm Mozambique Current (the southern branch of the equatorial current which hits Africa and splits) pushes southwards, forcing the eastern branch of the Benguela Current away from the coast.

What makes the Cape and Cape Point so interesting and varied climatically is that these two great currents, with an average temperature difference between them of 15°C, meet and pass at the finger-tip of the Cape Peninsula.

The Marine Suburbs

Thus the Atlantic coast of the Peninsula can be thought of as the 'cold side' and the sea on this coast tends to be clear and cold, with a variety of kelps and other seaweeds growing along the rocky shoreline. On a hot day, however, this cold water is very refreshing, and is said to discourage sharks, which prefer warmer water!

Between the city and the Atlantic stand Signal Hill and Lion's Head, and it is in the lee of these that some of the most sheltered suburbs in the Peninsula lie.

Going down the coast from Table Bay, one passes Mouille Point, where the oldest lighthouse in South Africa still operates.

Sea Point, with its blocks of flats right down to the beachfront, is popular with visitors and holiday-makers because of its beaches and lawns, and also its dazzling night-life.

Clifton is thought to have one of the most beautiful beaches in the world, with cottages spilling all over the steep slopes above its four coves.

Where Lion's Head meets the Twelve Apostles, there is a deep ravine or kloof called the Glen, a shady picnic area which also contains the Round House, a restaurant which was originally the hunting lodge of Lord Charles Somerset.

Camps Bay, on the slopes of the Twelve Apostles, was named after Frederick von Kamptz, who married the widow of the owner of the original farm, *Ravenstyn*. Prone to be windy, it overlooks a long straight beach whose currents are not altogether trustworthy, edged with lawns and a picnic area. There is a tidal pool in the rocks nearby.

Bakoven ('baking oven') was named for the huge domed rock in the sea there which has a large round hole in the side of it.

Above: Only two buildings can be seen in this old photograph of Clifton and Lion's Head, one of which is the Clifton Hotel. The promontory from which the photograph was taken is now crowded with bungalows and cottages. (Cape Archives)

From Bakoven the beautiful marine drive, Victoria Road, heads past the coves of Jack's Beach and Oudekraal towards Llandudno and Hout Bay.

Llandudno lies on the steep slopes of Little Lion's Head. The views from here are spectacular. The beach, however, has currents that are treacherous and many people prefer to walk along the coast past Sunset Rocks to the more sheltered Sandy Bay. Because this beach is secluded and isolated it is also popular with naturists and has achieved a certain notoriety as a 'nudist' beach. There is a move afoot to develop Sandy Bay as a built-up holiday resort, but it seems a pity to spoil one of the few remaining natural areas within easy reach of the city.

Beyond Sandy Bay is a promontory of rocks named Oudeschip, where local fishermen have built tiny driftwood shacks between the granite boulders in which they can live over weekends.

From Llandudno the road leads up to the nek between Little Lion's Head and Slangoolie, the last buttress of the Twelve Apostles, and over into Hout Bay, a peaceful and picturesque valley which is still partially farmed. The green valley sweeps down to the curving bay with its old fishing harbour, guarded by the majestic Sentinel Peak.

Beyond Hout Bay the road winds along the

cliff face on the magnificent Chapman's Peak Drive. This incredible road is cut into the rock where the Cape Granite and Table Mountain Sandstone layers meet, and was built between 1915 and 1922, with engineers and equipment sometimes having to reach the sites with the aid of climbing ropes!

The road drops down to Noordhoek, an isolated village clustered at the northern end of Long Beach which stretches 4 km to Kommetjie, another small village. Though fairly dangerous unless one knows the currents, this beach is popular for surfing.

From Kommetjie the road goes south past small bays such as Olifants Bay and

Scarborough, right down to Cape Point itself with its old stone lighthouse perched on the forbidding cliff at the foot of which the waters of the Atlantic and Indian Oceans restlessly surge.

The Southern Suburbs

Apart from the marine suburbs of the west coast, the main residential area of Cape Town is tucked away behind the city itself, in a string of suburbs along the eastern slopes of Devil's Peak and Table Mountain.

Woodstock and Observatory with their narrow streets and ramshackle houses are dominated by the Groote Schuur Hospital. Eastwards, further away from the mountain, lies

Pinelands, named the 'Garden City'.

Rondebosch, one of the oldest suburbs in Cape Town, is where the Vryburghers, soldiers released from service by Van Riebeeck, were alotted land to farm. The village is a hive of activity during university terms, but quietens down for the vacations. The University of Cape Town spreads across the slopes of Devil's Peak above Rondebosch in one of the most beautiful campus settings in the world.

Higher up, above Mowbray and overlooking the whole of the Cape Flats towards the Groot Drakenstein and Hottentots Holland mountains, is the Rhodes Memorial, designed by Sir Herbert Baker as a fitting tribute to the spirit of this great man. In the grounds of the memorial there is an old stone-and-thatch tearoom, and many pleasant walks can be taken in the area. Every year, the Salvation Army holds a service at the Rhodes Memorial on Easter Sunday, which is timed to end just as the sun rises over the mountains of the Boland.

Newlands has one of the highest average rainfalls in the Cape and its gardens are lush and green. The oaks lining Newlands Avenue were amongst the first trees to be planted in the Peninsula, and still burst forth in young, fresh green every spring.

On the slopes of Table Mountain above Newlands is the Kirstenbosch National Botanic Garden, established in 1913 by Professor Harold Pearson for the collection, preservation and study of the indigenous flora of Southern Africa. Its work has been internationally recognised, and its beautifully maintained grounds are always a delight to wander in.

The adjoining rugby and cricket grounds in Newlands have an international reputation, and the cricket ground in particular is considered one of the prettiest to be seen, with its oak trees and mountain views.

Claremont has become the shopping centre of the southern suburbs, with several large, modern shopping complexes and many small, interesting shops in its side streets. Many residents find it easier to shop in the southern suburbs than to go into the city itself, because of parking difficulties.

Upper Claremont and Bishopscourt are sheltered residential areas with beautifully laid-out private homes.

Wynberg is another very old suburb with a distinctly English flavour – it was here that the British established a military camp and hospital when they first occupied the Cape, and the English officers and their wives lived in Wynberg. Many mementoes of the era remain, particularly in the 'Chelsea' area of Wynberg.

This area also boasts an open-air theatre in Maynardville Park, where a season of Shakespeare is presented annually.

Southwards from Wynberg towards False Bay, along the slopes of Table Mountain and Constantiaberg, lies a large semi-rural district known as Constantia. This area is strongly associated with the Cape Dutch tradition and the Cape wine industry, as it was in this ideal environment for viticulture that the Dutch first built farm homesteads in the 'Cape Dutch' style and settled down to develop wines which have become world-renowned.

Many of these old homesteads are still perfectly preserved, and one of the most famous of these is Groot Constantia, built in 1685 by Simon van der Stel. It is a typical example of a Cape Dutch homestead, and many of the original furnishings may still be seen there. Behind the house are the dark and gloomy slave quarters and the large wine cellar, in which Constantia wines are still produced.

South of Constantia lies the Tokai Forest, with its walks and picnic areas, while in the mountains overlooking Tokai and Muizenberg is the Silvermine Nature Reserve. This large reserve has scenic walks, drives and picnic areas, and many indigenous plant species are to be seen. The entrance to the reserve is at the crest of the Old Cape Road, which winds over the mountain pass between Tokai and Noordhoek.

Further away from the mountain, towards the False Bay coast, lie several shallow expanses of water known as 'vleis'. Zeekoevlei is popular for sailing. Rondevlei has been declared a bird sanctuary, while part of Sandvlei has been developed as a marina.

Muizenberg, an area which used to be very popular, especially with visitors from the Transvaal, is now a neglected suburb, though the long beach, which shelves gradually into the warm water of the Indian Ocean, is still popular for swimming and surfing, when the south-east wind is not blowing.

The mountains rise very sharply on this side of the Peninsula, so that the houses are restricted to a narrow belt along the coast.

Beyond Muizenberg, St James is a pretty suburb with a small beach, tidal pool and brightly painted beach huts.

Kalk Bay still has a busy fishing harbour and some of the picturesque fishermen's cottages have survived.

Fish Hoek was originally one estate granted to Andries Bruins in 1818 on condition that no public house was kept there, and this teetotal state is still perpetuated in the modern town. Another condition that still holds is that fishing rights here are totally unreserved. The beach is

Right: The small cottage in Muizenberg where Cecil John Rhodes died. (Cape Archives)

Kalk Bay harbour at the turn of the century. (Cape Archives)

also popular for swimming and boating.

Simonstown, the end of the railway line which runs right next to the shore, is a substantial town which was first developed as a naval base in 1814 by the British, and it remained a Royal Naval Base until 1957, when it was handed over to the South African Navy.

South of Simonstown, there are several small bays and beaches, such as Seaforth, Boulders, Miller's Point, Smitswinkel Bay and Buffels Bay, before one finally reaches Cape Point.

FURTHER AFIELD

Cape Flats

Between the Cape Peninsula and the first mountain ranges of the interior lie the Cape Flats, a 40 km expanse of sand, which 60 million years ago was a shallow stretch of water separating the island with the flat-topped mountain from the mainland.

On the Flats lie the northern suburbs of Cape Town. These include the industrial areas such as Paarden Eiland and Epping; the suburbs stretching up the coast such as Milnerton and Table View; and the districts of Goodwood, Parow, Bellville and Durbanville, with their satellite suburbs, which were once separate towns, but, as the city expanded in such directions as the mountain allowed, they became absorbed into what is known as 'Greater Cape Town'.

Also on the Flats are the Coloured suburbs such as Bonteheuwel, Ottery, Lotus River, Grassy Park and Retreat; and further east, the

Simonstown in 1860. (Cape Archives)

African townships such as Langa, Nyanga and Guguletu.

There is an acute shortage of housing for non-whites in Cape Town, and in order to combat this, a large township called Mitchell's Plain has been built some 30 km out of town – but transport costs are very high in these days of fuel crisis, and this necessarily discourages people from living so far away from their work.

Another result of the housing shortage is the mushrooming of squatter camps – where people have erected colonies of tin shanties on any open ground. From time to time the authorities have insisted on demolishing these illegal shanty towns, but this is not a constructive solution to the problem.

Sandveld

From the shores of Blouberg and Melkboschstrand on the west coast there is an uninterrupted view of Table Mountain across Table Bay. Higher up and slightly inland are Mamre, a rural village which has grown up around the Moravian mission station established in 1808, and Darling, a village which is one of the centres of the glorious spring wildflower displays. There is a flower reserve near Darling, as well as two private farms, Waylands and Oudepos, which are open to visitors viewing the flowers.

The small coastal villages of Ysterfontein and Churchhaven are visited by Capetonians looking for a quiet holiday or weekend out of the city.

Saldanha Bay and Langebaan are also popular resorts with boating and fishing. Saldanha Bay is a natural harbour with its deep but sheltered water. The bay is harvested for guano (on the islands) and seaweed. Langebaan Lagoon is connected to Saldanha Bay by a narrow channel, and teems with fish and bird life.

Boland

North-east of Cape Town lies the Boland. It was in this direction that the first expansion of the original Dutch colony took place, and the earliest inland settlements developed here, such as Stellenbosch, founded in 1680 by Simon van der Stel, Paarl and Franschhoek, settled by the French Huguenots after their arrival in 1688.

The main road that runs north-east out of Cape Town is known as the Great North Road, or the Cape to Cairo Road, and in these early stages it runs through Paarl, which was named for the great granite dome of rock behind it which glistens like a pearl in the rain. Nearby is built the simple but effective monument to the Afrikaans language which overlooks the whole of the Berg River Valley towards the Groot Drakenstein mountains and Simonsberg.

The Great North Road continues over the Du Toit's Kloof Pass, which winds 48 km through the mountains, at one stage tunnelling through the living rock for a short distance, before descending to the Breë River Valley, and the town of Worcester. Nearby are the lovely Karoo Gardens, a stunning sight in spring, and the Goudini Spa, a health resort with hot mineral springs.

If one branches north-west at Paarl, there is another route through the mountain, over the Bain's Kloof Pass. This scenic pass offers easy access to the mountains for hiking and camping, or picnicking at the Witte River, just below the road, over the crest of the pass.

Another short pass, Michell's Pass, and the road drops down to Ceres, in the southernmost part of the Cold Bokkeveld. Ceres, as its name implies, is the heart of a thriving fruit-farming area. The surrounding mountains are popular for hiking and camping. In winter, when snow falls, there is skiing on the mountains surrounding the valley, a rare thing in the Cape.

The towns of Wolseley and Tulbagh (once known as 'The Land of Waveren') were much damaged in the earth tremors of 1969. Many of

Right: Victoria Road, between Camps Bay and Llandudno, at the turn of the century. (Cape Archives)

Below: The old Pastorie at Tulbagh. (Cape Archives)

the old buildings in Tulbagh have now been restored as nearly as possible to their original state, and are preserved as national monuments. Of particular interest is the old Drostdy, or magisterial residence, of Tulbagh, designed by Louis-Michel Thibault, which now houses a period museum.

At the feet of the Groot Drakenstein mountains and Stellenboschberg, is the historic town of Stellenbosch, with its oak-lined streets and dignified Cape Dutch buildings. The town, conscious of its heritage, has preserved many of the old buildings as museums, and one of the most interesting is the Stellenryck Wine Museum.

In the mountains behind Stellenbosch is Jonkershoek, a nature reserve and forest station with spectacular mountain walks and a pleasant picnic area.

Stellenbosch and Paarl are at the heart of the Cape Winelands. Many of the beautiful, historic farms of the 'wine route' welcome visitors with tours of the wine cellars and generous glasses of wine to taste.

Franschhoek, with its Huguenot memorial and pretty holiday farms, nestles behind the Groot Drakenstein mountains. From here the Franschhoek Pass leads over the Franschhoek mountains to the pretty, agricultural town of Villiersdorp, which lies peacefully in the midst of orchards and vineyards.

The other main road leading eastwards out of Cape Town runs closer to the south-east coast, going past the coastal towns of Somerset West and the Strand, before climbing Sir Lowry's Pass with its spectacular view of the whole Peninsula and Cape Flats from the summit. On the other side of the pass, the apple-growing district is centred round the town of Grabouw.

The road goes through the Houwhoek Pass, past Caledon with its museum and wild flower reserve and continues eastward along the Garden Route.

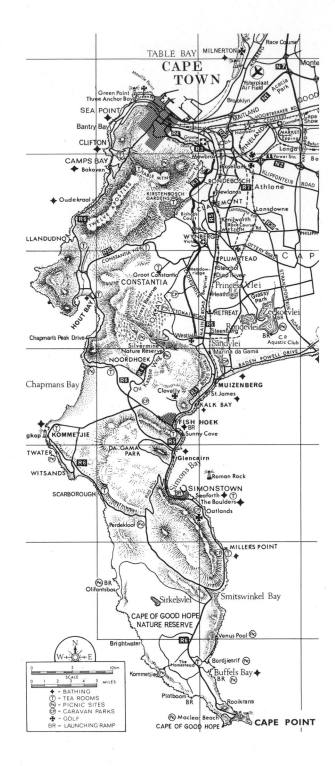

Overberg West

The great sweep of False Bay ends at Gordon's Bay and the promontory of Cape Hangklip. A narrow road winds all along the very edge of the coast, past the little villages such as Pringle Bay, Rooi Els and Betty's Bay, where there is a beautifully laid-out botanical garden.

Kleinmond is on the western side of the mouth of the Kleinmond Lagoon, round which the road detours before returning to the coast and the villages of Hawston and Onrus along the way to Hermanus, a popular and yet not overcrowded holiday resort with pleasant beaches and a lagoon for boating and sailing.

In conclusion

An introduction can only mention some of the fascinating aspects of the City of Cape Town and its surrounding environs, and hardly scratches the surface of the scenic wonder and historical interest of the South Western Cape. What gives that dynamic spark, however, is that it is all here, the people to be met and the places to be explored. It is beauty and life, happening now.

Left: Map of the Cape Peninsula. (Captour)

Below: Map of the South-western Cape. (Captour)

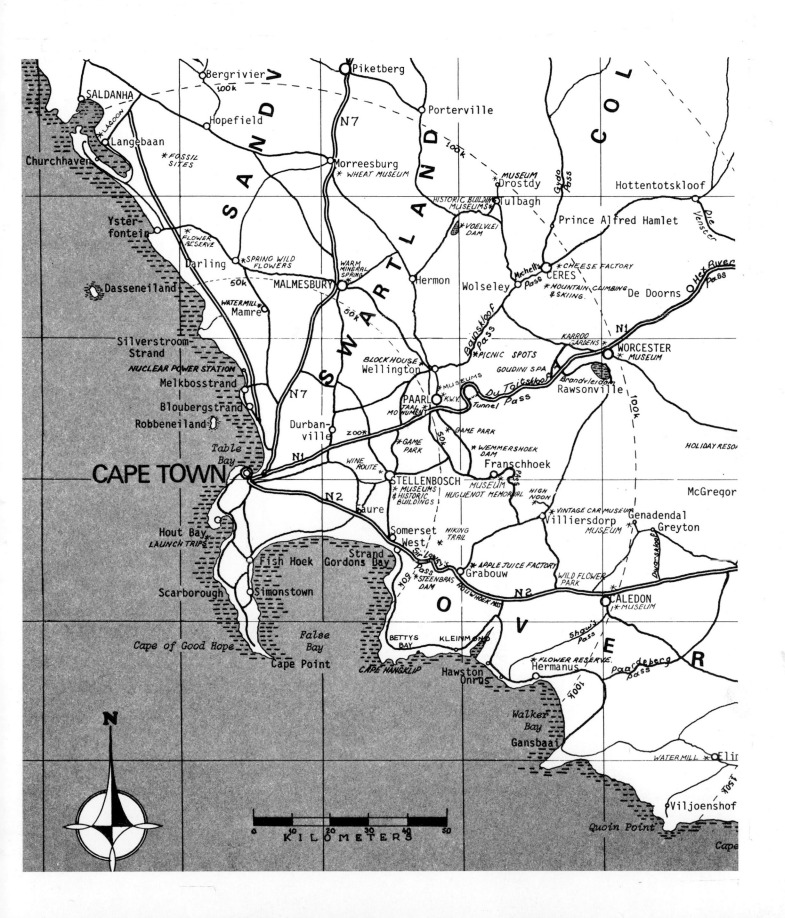

1 The lights of the city and harbour –
a scattering of bright gems.

2 The old-fashioned tugboat, *H. Sawyer*, which used to pilot vessels in and out of Cape Town harbour, is now stationed at Luderitz in Namibia.

3 Kloof Corner and the upper cable station, at the western end of the front table of Table Mountain, seen from Signal Hill.

4 Spring flowers on the slopes of Signal Hill, looking towards Lion's Head.

2

3

5

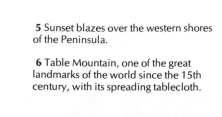

5 Sunset blazes over the western shores of the Peninsula.

6 Table Mountain, one of the great landmarks of the world since the 15th century, with its spreading tablecloth.

6

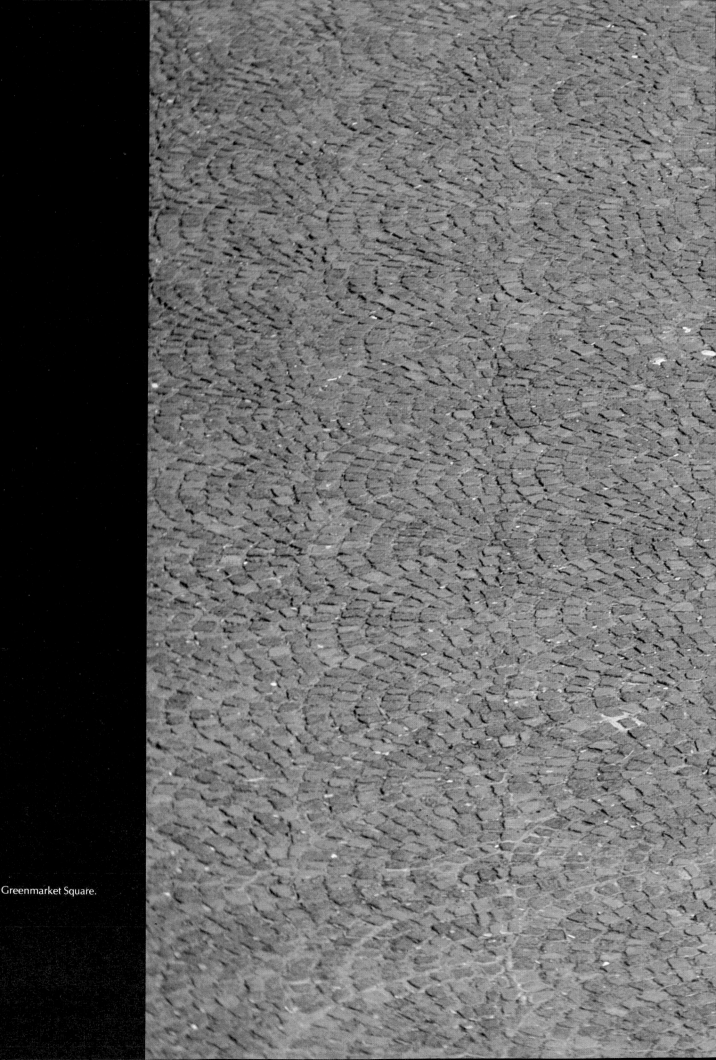

Greenmarket Square.

8 Doing maintenance work on the Table Mountain Aerial Cableway gives one a bird's-eye view of the city.

9 One of the older sections of Cape Town harbour.

10 The fountain at the bottom of Adderley Street, where the Fresh River used to reach the sea.

11 Camps Bay lies in the lee of Lion's Head, seen here from Table Mountain.

12 The contrast of old and new: the Victoria and Albert
Pub, foregrounded against the monolithic B.P. Centre.

13 Still life with sunset and unfinished freeway.

13

14

15

14 The Blue Lodge, a charmingly ornate Victorian building in upper Long Street.

15 The new railway station in Adderley Street has outer murals of mosaic and attractive surrounding gardens.

16 A Victorian commercial house, built at the turn of the century.

17 A climber's paradise – but these cliffs can also be ascended by aerial cableway. View from the lower to the upper cable station.

18 An overalled workman paints the ogive windows of the Groote Kerk, the mother church of the Dutch Reformed Church in South Africa, rebuilt in 1779. The clock tower dates from 1703.

19 The main entrance of the Houses of Parliament, completed in 1884.

20 The Reserve Bank building in St George's Street, completed in 1976, is much admired for its austere lines.

21 Escalators at one of the entrances to the Strand Concourse, a multi-level underground shopping area in the city centre.

22

23

22 The old Customs House in Buitenkant Street, which was once used as a granary. It has a pediment with the British coat of arms, and is now used by the Public Works Department.

23 The entrance to the Castle of Good Hope, with the arms of the Dutch East India Company on the pediment.

24 The 'Kat' balcony in the Castle, scene of ceremonial occasions, was designed by Anton Anreith.

25 Bargain hunting at the open-air market on the Grand Parade.

26 The Grand Parade, once a military parade ground, is overlooked by the City Hall, built in 1905.

27 Overleaf: Sydney Harpley's statue of General J. C. Smuts is set in an open area of the old Company Gardens. In the background is the National Art Gallery, donated to the city by Hyman Libermann, a former mayor of Cape Town.

25

28 Looking up from the statue of Bartholomew Diaz towards Adderley Street, the commercial centre of the city.

29 A bright modernistic sculpture at the entrance to Shell House, Riebeek Street.

30 A second-hand stall under the wing (so to speak) of St George's Cathedral, facing onto Wale Street.

31 Reflections in the glass doors of the B.P. Centre down on the Foreshore.

30

29

31

32 A flag parade inaugurates an international gymnastics meeting held in the Grand Hall of the ultra-modern Good Hope Centre, completed in 1977.

33 Overleaf, left: 'One rand the bunch, Merrem!'

34 Overleaf, right: The tomb of the Moslem leader, Tuan Syed, on top of Signal Hill, is a *kramat* or shrine.

35 Yachts in the yacht basin down at Cape Town harbour.

36 The unmistakable cry of these coloured boys was originally supposed to represent the name of the paper they were offering.

37 The hothouse in the Botanical Gardens, which were originally established by Van Riebeeck to provide fresh fruit and vegetables for passing vessels.

38 The lower entrance to Government Avenue, between the Houses of Parliament and St George's Cathedral.

36

37

38

39
40

39 The Nico Malan Theatre and Opera House complex, built on reclaimed land down on the Foreshore.

40 Midday and the noon gun is fired from the slopes of Signal Hill. The site of the cannon has been used as an observation and signal post since the earliest times.

41 One of the old school: a tailor in Long Street.

42 A Malay flower seller on the Grand Parade.

43 Victorian cast iron railings and pillars on a balcony in upper Long Street.

44 The statue of General J. C. Smuts outside the Houses of Parliament was sculpted by the late Ivan Mitford-Barberton of Hout Bay, and erected in 1973.

45 The Offices of the State President: part of the Tuynhuys.

45

46
47

48

49

50

52

51

53

54

46 The *Zinatul Islam* mosque in Muir Street, District Six.

47 Minaret of the Ellesmere Road mosque, District Six.

48 Inside the *Zinatul Islam* mosque.

49 One of the minarets of the *Zinatul Islam* mosque.

50 The *Masjid Kuatal* mosque in Loop Street, which was built in about 1880.

51-54 Scenes from a Malay wedding.

51 The bride in her finery.

52 The bridegroom kneels in the mosque.

53 The bride does not go to the mosque, but is represented by her father. After the ceremony the bridegroom returns to the bride's house and places the ring on her finger, after which the celebration begins.

54 Father and bridegroom embrace.

56

55 District Six, on the slopes of Devil's Peak.

56 Sign of the times.

57 Colourful washing and people hang from a balcony
in District Six.

58 'Ja, I live here.'

59

60

61

59 Crumbling walls – age and decay do their work.

60 Graffiti.

61 White-robed Moslem children return from the mosque.

62 Camera-shy children of District Six.

63 A Moslem child wearing the traditional *kofiya*.

64 Typical flat-roofed Georgian houses of the Malay Quarter.

65 The seafront promenade at Sea Point.

66 Yachts off Mouille Point.

64

67 Blocks of flats overlooking the beachfront at Three Anchor Bay.

68 The President Hotel at the Bantry Bay end of Sea Point, below Lion's Head.

69 The Mouille Point lighthouse, oldest in South Africa,

70 Bantry Bay – a corruption of the name 'Botany Bay'. Herbs and plants were grown there for medicinal purposes by the early settlers.

68

69

73

74

75

73 A crowded afternoon on 4th beach, Clifton.

74 Soaking up sunshine on the west coast.

75 Granite boulders at Clifton.

76 Yachts anchored in the bay off Clifton beach.

77 Not the ghost ship *The Flying Dutchman* but the Argentinian training ship *Libertad* sails out of Table Bay.

78 Camps Bay, dominated by the buttresses of the Twelve Apostles.

79 The grassed picnic area between trees and granite boulders at Camps Bay beach.

80 The bowling greens at Camps Bay – set between sea and mountain.

81 Sunbathing – the most popular summer sport in Cape Town.

79

80

82 The Greek tanker *Romelia* drifted on to Sunset Rocks,
Llandudno, in April 1977.

83 Llandudno, on the steep slopes of Little Lion's Head,
with Karbonkelberg in the background.

84 Hout Bay beach.

85

88

85 Looking back towards Hout Bay from the Chapman's Peak Drive.

86 *Kronendal,* in Hout Bay, built at the beginning of the 19th century, now houses a restaurant equipped with period furnishings.

87 The *Circe,* a privately owned launch, runs sight-seeing cruises from Hout Bay to Table Bay.

88 Waiting on the Hout Bay quayside for the snoek boats to come in.

89

90

91

89 Colourful fishing floats.

90 Oil-skinned Hout Bay fishermen.

91 Fishing boats lie at their moorings in Hout Bay harbour.

92

93

92 Chapman's Peak Drive, built between 1915 and 1922, is cut into the rock at the junction of the Cape Granite and Table Mountain Sandstone layers.

93 Baboons frequent the Chapman's Peak Drive. In general there are few large wild animals to be seen in the Peninsula.

94 Long Beach, Noordhoek.

95 Hout Bay's green valley.

96 Scarborough, a small village south of Kommetjie on the west coast of the Peninsula.

97 The steel tower of Slangkop lighthouse at Kommetjie.

98 Kommetjie faces across Chapman's Bay to Chapman's Peak and Hout Bay.

96

98

99 Yachts on Zeekoevlei.

100 A restored house in Wolfe Street, Wynberg, which now houses an antique shop.

101 The Dutch Reformed Church, Church Street, Wynberg, was built in 1831.

102 Restored cottages in the 'Chelsea' area of Wynberg.

103 *Clarence*, Victoria Road, Wynberg.

104 Paradise Road, Newlands, looking up towards Fernwood Peak and Ascension Buttress.

105 Kirstenbosch in spring, looking up towards Castle Rock.

106 Starry white *Dimorphotheca* daisies.

107 A clump of bright orange *Gazania*.

108 *Romulea rosea*, or 'Froetang'.

109 One of the many succulent 'vygies', *Lampranthus aurea*.

110 The *Strelitzia*, or 'crane flower'.

111 The delicate flower of *Drosera*, the insectivorous Sun-dew plant.

112 Sun-loving wild flax, *Heliophila coronopifolia*.

113 *Leucospermum nutans* – the Pincushion protea.

114 The 'Candelabra flower', *Brunsvigia orientalis*.

115 *Babiana*, commonly called 'bobbejaantjie', because baboons greedily eat the bulbs.

116 *Protea cynaroides*, the King protea, is a national emblem.

118

117 The lily pond at the Kirstenbosch National Botanic Gardens.

118 A display of white watsonias in the rockery in front of the tearoom at Kirstenbosch.

119 The reservoir at the Silvermine Nature Reserve.

120 The wine cellar of the historic homestead Groot Constantia, with its ornamental pediment by the celebrated German sculptor, Anton Anreith.

119

120

122

123

121 Constantia valley.

122 The facade of the Groot Constantia homestead.

123 A well-formed bunch of Shiraz grapes. Groot Constantia is famous for its estate wines.

124 One of the Groot Constantia vineyards.

124

125 Fallow deer, *Dama dama,* in the grounds of the Rhodes Memorial.

126 Rhodes Memorial, designed by Sir Herbert Baker in 1912.

127 Groote Schuur Hospital, built on ground bequeathed to the nation by Cecil John Rhodes.

125

127

128 *Groote Schuur* itself, the residence originally built as a barn in 1657 and restored for Rhodes by Sir Herbert Baker in 1897. Rhodes bequeathed it to the nation and it has been the official prime minister's residence ever since.

129 Mostert's Mill on the old farm Welgelegen is the only surviving windmill in Cape Town.

130 The Cape's premier race meeting, the 'Met' (Metropolitan Stakes), at the Kenilworth race course.

130

131

132

133

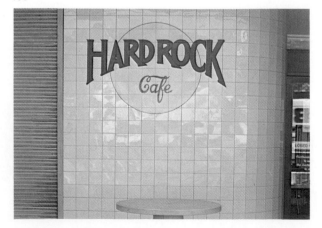

134

132 This Victorian lamp post was the first street light in the Peninsula. It was installed in 1886 and fed by current supplied by the private plant owned by D. Pigot-Moodie, who had presented the fountain and drinking trough for horses to the Rondebosch Municipality.

133 Entrance to a Rondebosch restaurant.

134 Rondebosch Common, an open public area, which was once used as a parade and drilling ground by Batavian troops. In the background, the University of Cape Town is spread across the slopes of Devil's Peak.

135

136

135-137 The 'Coon Carnival' traditionally takes place on 2nd January, known as 'Tweede Nuwejaar'. The brightly costumed troupes parade through to the Hartleyvale stadium where competitions for the best turned-out and most accomplished bands are held.

137

138-139 Fruit and vegetables at the Salt River market.

138

139

140 Table Mountain from the shores of Bloubergstrand.

141 The cliffs of Cape Point.

142 Overleaf: An aerial view of Cape Point at the tip of the Cape Peninsula.

140

143

144

145

143 Buffels Bay, looking towards Cape Point.

144 The naval base of Simonstown.

145 Colourful sails of the Hobie cats (small catamarans) at Fish Hoek beach.

146 Fishermen at Kalk Bay.

147 The tidal pool at St James.

148 Line-caught Red Roman.

149 The beach at Muizenberg stretches into the distance.

150 Overleaf: Early morning light at Kalk Bay.

148

147

151

151 Marina da Gama, a housing complex on Sandvlei.

152 Long rollers at Strandfontein, looking back towards Muizenberg.

153-155 The Crossroads squatter camp out near D. F. Malan airport on the Cape Flats.

152

155

156 Church at Pniel, near Stellenbosch.   **157** Farm dam near Stellenbosch.

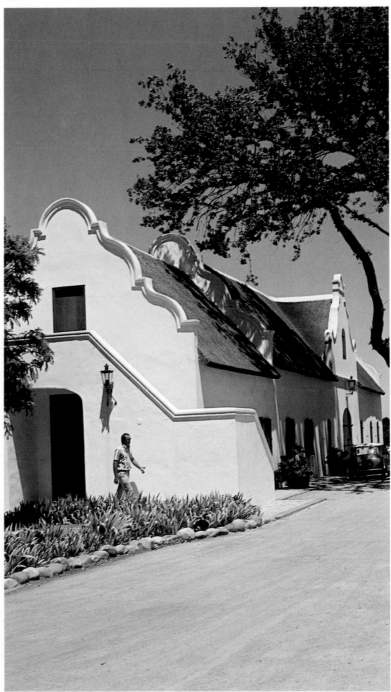

158 *Libertas Parva* (Rembrandt van Rijn Art Centre), a portion of the original farm *Libertas* in Stellenbosch, was built in about 1783.

159 Interior of the Stellenryck Wine Museum, Stellenbosch.

160 End gable of the Stellenryck Wine Museum.

161 The homestead of *Lanzerac*, built in 1830, is now used as a hotel.

162 A restored Cape Dutch cottage in Stellenbosch,
shaded by Simon van der Stel's beloved oak trees.

164

163

163 The old slave bell at *Lanzerac,* near Stellenbosch.

164 Peach blossom in the spring.

165 The parsonage of the Rhenish Mission Church.

166 The *Kruithuis,* or Powder Magazine, on the open ground of the Braak in Stellenbosch, has a bell tower and a domed roof of clinker tiles. In its arsenal are old cannon and weapons used in the Battle of Blouberg in 1806.

167

167 Farm labourer of the Boland.

168 The homestead of *Nederburg* near Stellenbosch, which has become famous for the quality of the estate wine produced here.

169 Old German wine press outside the Stellenryck Wine Museum, Stellenbosch.

170 *Old Nectar,* another historic Cape Dutch homestead at Jonkershoek near Stellenbosch, is now the home of Una van der Spuy, an authority on Cape flora.

168

169

171 Picnicking at Jonkershoek.

172 *La Dauphine*, Franschhoek.

173 Winter, and snow caps the mountain ranges of the Boland.

174 The Huguenot Memorial at Franschhoek, erected in honour of the French immigrants who settled in the area in the 17th century.

175 Snow on the Franschhoek Pass. The road through the pass was built in 1824.

176

177

178

179

176 Berg River Valley, Paarl.

177 Entrance to the head office of the KWV
(*Ko-operatiewe Wynbouers Vereeniging*) in Paarl.

178 Steep mountains flanking the Du Toit's Kloof Pass.

179 Autumn vineyard near Paarl.

180 Overleaf, left: A patchwork of vineyards in the Hex
River Valley.

181 Overleaf, right: Vivid spring flowers in the Karoo
Gardens near Worcester.

183

182

182 After the earth tremors in 1969, many of the damaged cottages in Tulbagh were restored to their original 18th century appearance.

183 The interior of the *Drostdy* or magisterial residence at Tulbagh, which was designed by Louis-Michel Thibault.

184 The whole of the restored main street of Tulbagh has been declared a national monument.

185 The town of Tulbagh.

184

186

187

186 The lagoon at Langebaan, frequented by fish and bird life. Below the surface of the water is a vast deposit of oyster shell, used in the manufacture of lime.

187 A field of spring flowers near Darling.

188 Mellow autumn colouring in a vineyard near Du Toit's Kloof Pass.

189 Steenbras Dam near the summit of Sir Lowry's Pass. There is an attractive camping area beside the dam.

190 Gordon's Bay.

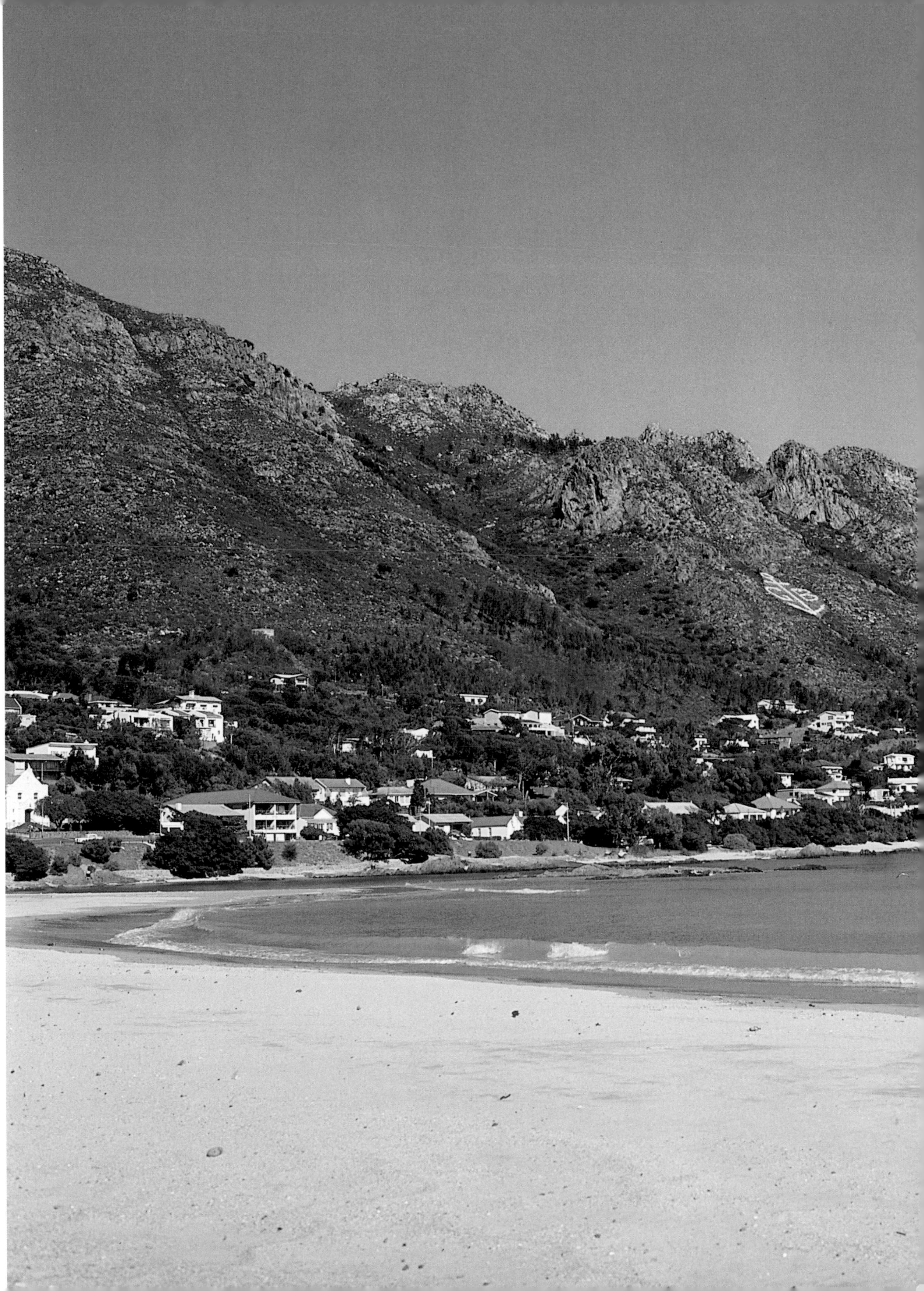

191

192

191 The road to Cape Hangklip.

192 Small craft harbour, Gordon's Bay.

193 The coastal resort of Hermanus.

194 Green farmlands near Caledon

193

194

195

196

195 The curving marks of contour ploughing near Caledon.

196 A field of spring flowers at the Caledon Gardens.

197 The Caledon Gardens were founded in 1927 and laid out by a landscape gardener named Cecil Young in 1933.

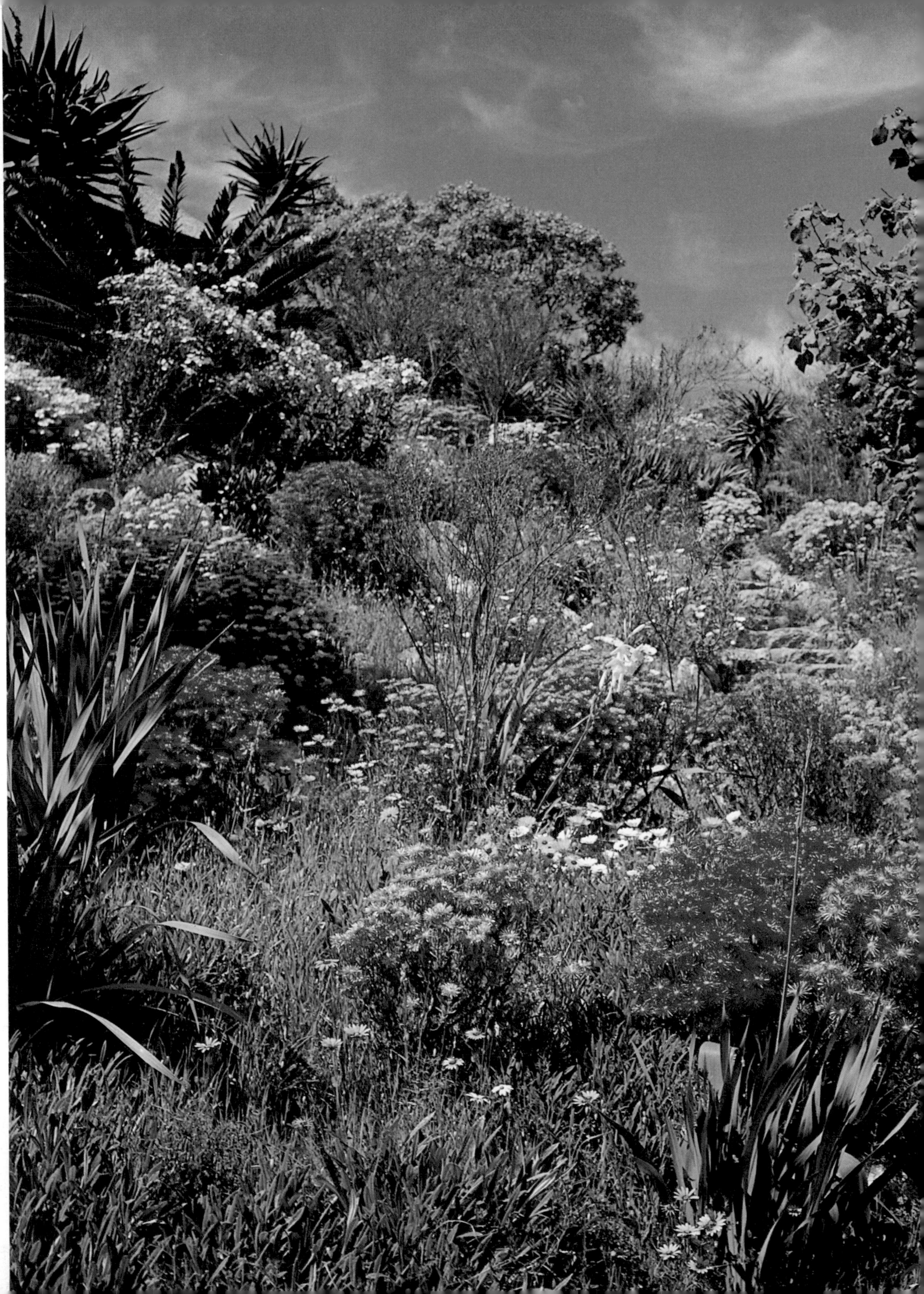

LIST OF PHOTOGRAPHIC SOURCES

Captour:
9, 10, 11, 20, 23, 40, 66, 73, 74, 76, 79, 84, 87, 117, 119, 125, 142, 159, 171, 179, 181, 183, 194, 196, 197.

Farley, Geraldine:
26, 51, 52, 53, 54, 65, 69, 82, 90, 110, 129, 131, 132, 133, 138, 146, 147, 148, 153, 154.

Griffiths, Glynn:
Jacket, 1, 7, 8, 12, 13, 14, 16, 18, 21, 22, 25, 27, 29, 30, 31, 32, 33, 36, 37, 38, 41, 43, 83, 136, 150, 155.

Lindenberg, Paul:
46, 47, 48, 49, 55, 56, 59, 60, 61.

All the other colour photographs were taken by Jean Morris.